Marilyn MONROE

Marilyn MONROE

TOM HUTCHINSON

Exeter Books

NEW YORK

Photographic acknowledgments

All photographs published in this book are from the Kobal Collection, London, with the exception of the following: Camera Press, London 66 top, 66 below, 67; Central Press, London 7, 42; Colour Library International, London 59, 75; Popperfoto, London 9 top, 43, 52, 64, 68, 78; Rex Features 6, 8, 12, 19, 21, 25, 34, 44, 49, 50, 61 top, 73, 74 below, 77.

Front cover: Kobal Collection.
Back cover: *Gentlemen Prefer Blondes* (Twentieth Century-Fox). Kobal Collection.
Frontispiece: *There's No Business like Show Business* (Twentieth Century-Fox). Kobal Collection.

CONTENTS

NORMA JEAN

The uncomplicated glamour of one of the screen's last and most potent love goddesses, Marilyn Monroe.

She was the girl who had everything – and nothing. She had all to live for, yet her death was called 'probable suicide'. She, who could have had her pick of any man in the world, died alone on a Saturday night – the night when everyone had a date. Everyone that is apart from her.

All her life Marilyn Monroe was a paradox, a contradiction in the terms that Hollywood set her. She was the most famous sex symbol in the world, a blonde bombshell detonating in all men's dreams as an implication of attainable femininity. Yet there was an interior innocence about her which, like a watermark, gleamed through that surface gloss of glamour.

She came on with the presence of royalty. When I first saw her she had arrived in London to make *The Prince and the Showgirl* with Laurence Olivier, and they sat on a dais at the end of the hotel's banqueting room inviting questions from the assembled Pressmen, for all the world as though the two of them were Government officials or statesmen. Other stars would hold receptions at which they mingled with journalists, but Olivier and Monroe were just that bit above that sort of thing. It was not so much condescension, as the natural order of things.

During the filming of *The Prince and the Showgirl* I met her a couple of times, in more intimate circumstances, at the house she had rented just outside London. There were always 'courtiers' around, of course; often, she said, she relied on them to make her decisions for her. Often they would answer for her, and she would look blankly on, like a ventriloquist's beautiful doll that has forgotten its lines.

Looking back at her too-short life, it does seem that too rarely did she write her own lines: she always appeared dependent upon others. Yet in her movies how different a character, how self-sufficient and, even, self-mocking, she could be, with those pouting lips and that bottom-wiggle.

By her movies shall we know her: that style, that languorous, aware personality, that sense of wit. Even in films that might be termed disaster areas, she was always a saving grace, by very virtue of being in them in the first place. We felt her vulnerability as though it were a physical atmosphere; instinctively we were always on her side. In *The Asphalt Jungle* she plays the young mistress of the much older Louis Calhern, who is involved with a robbery. 'Some sweet kid'

Marilyn Monroe at a press conference at the Savoy Hotel, London, in 1956, when she came to England to make *The Prince and the Showgirl*. Lighting a cigarette for her is her co-star, perhaps the world's greatest actor, Sir Laurence Olivier, and to the left is her husband, one of the world's leading playwrights, Arthur Miller.

is his comment on her, meant without sarcasm. It was always how we thought of her.

The end of a life usually means the end of a career, the celebrity lingering on in the minds and rituals only of the faithful adherents, as in the cases of Elvis Presley and James Dean. Paradoxically, it seems that Marilyn's aftermath has added fresh impetus to the interest in her. Biographies have been written either as straightforward accounts or, most notoriously in the case of Norman Mailer, as *faction*. Films have been made around her life with look-alike Marilyns. The public interest in her is still at peak point. Why should this be so?

It is given to some rare ones to become myths while they are still alive, but Marilyn has become a legend after her death. This may be because we sense in her that inno-

cence I spoke of, that quality of allure combined with an unknowing sensuality. She gave her films a sense of occasion that still survives no matter how many times we see them on television or up there on the bigger screen. Our continuing interest is because we sense in her some of the contradictions within ourselves: the difference between what we think we are and what others see.

Marilyn's life and career spelt out that difference between the image and the imaginer. She has been called one of the last great romantic figures of the screen, but we know that behind that romantic ideal was a woman who was far different from that outward conception. That, unconsciously, we understand and sympathize with. Marilyn Monroe was all things to men and to women. Yet she was just the one thing with which they could all identify. That is her paradox. That is why her legend is indestructible.

On 1 June 1926 the talk at Consolidated Film Industries in Hollywood was about the absence of Gladys Mortensen. Gladys was a section head in the firm, which spliced film together for the principal studios; she was as liked as any other boss would be, but perhaps there was a touch of malice to spike the gossip with a sense of how are the mighty fallen. For Gladys was not at work because she was having a baby and she wasn't married to the man who was reputed to be the father: one of the firm's junior executives.

Gladys had been married once and already had two children, who were living with relatives, but she was now single and fancy-free. That fancy, though, was now no longer as free, but was tethered to a hospital bed as she gave birth to a little girl, Norma Jean,

The Hollywood film-cutter's daughter who became a legend with the superstar of an earlier generation, Alan Ladd.

the girl who was to become Marilyn Monroe. Marilyn herself never liked the name of Norma: 'I think I was christened it because Norma was a very box-office name around that time, what with Norma Shearer, that sort of thing. But it sounded too Normal, if you know what I mean.'

The name, though, was typical of Gladys's addiction to the movies; she was star-struck in the most infatuated of ways. She would have liked to have been on screen herself, but Consolidated Film Industries was the nearest she got to that ambition. There was a time when Marilyn – as she later told 'The King' himself – believed that Clark Gable was her real father. That was something that Gladys had hinted at, perhaps hoping that the wish was father to the need . . .

Norma Jean was a normal, rather podgy baby whose first experience of maternal love was to find herself farmed out to some friends of her mother, the Bolenders, in Hawthorne in the suburb of Los Angeles. Her mother had to return to work, but would visit Norma Jean 'every Saturday'.

That unsettled childhood pattern of being fostered out was to be repeated over and over again throughout her childhood. 'I never had real family', she later recalled, 'although my mother did try her best.' Certainly Gladys was regular with her payments – 25 dollars a month – for Norma Jean's upkeep, and her Saturday visits were welcomed eagerly by the little girl. The visits of her grandmother, Della, had also been looked forward to. But suddenly they stopped. The reason was that Della had been committed to a State Mental Institution, a fact which caused Gladys much disquiet about her own mental condition.

Della's incarceration came about after a period when she was much given to losing her temper and throwing things. Once, she was said to have tried to kill Norma Jean, who was just over 18 months old. She had asked the Bolenders if she could look after the baby for an afternoon. Marilyn later recalled: 'I remember waking up from my nap fighting for my life. Something was pressed against my face. It could have been a pillow. I fought with all my strength.' It seems that Della suddenly became aware of what she was doing and stopped trying to suffocate the child. Marilyn was never to forget it.

It seems that from the moment of her mother's institutionalization, Gladys's depressions, which were already quite profound, got worse. Her father had similarly been confined in a mental hospital and her brother, Marion, had also been stricken with the same illness. She herself felt 'marked out', as she put it.

Then, in 1933, she felt able to bring Norma Jean to live with her in her North

Hollywood home, a large part of which she had rented out to an English couple who worked in and out of films. There Norma Jean learned a wholly different way of life from that of the religious Bolenders, for the talk now was of the gossip of the studios: who was dating whom among the stars, who was up for which role in which movie. The showbiz trade paper, *Variety,* was the new bible which Norma Jean learned to accept with as much enjoyment as the former real Bible which the Bolenders had in their front room.

Norma Jean did all the things which little girls at her age did, and the Great Depression certainly did not concern her overmuch. She noticed that the corners were occupied by people lounging around, looking for something to do; it certainly never occurred to her that they were out of work. Then one day calamity struck her in a way that, ever after, she was to maintain, made her 'a natural victim'. Her mother Gladys was committed to a mental hospital. Her hysterias had been getting worse; the neighbours had complained: strait-jacketed and raving she was taken away. When Marilyn came home from school she was told: 'Your mother's gone away for a time.' In recent months Gladys had been working as a film cutter for Columbia Studios and for some weeks the Studios kept on paying her salary. But that dried up eventually. Late in 1935, Norma Jean was admitted to the Los Angeles Orphan Home Society.

She remembered her nearly two years there with some bitterness, but in fact it appears that conditions were not deliberately cruel or brutal; it was just that, being a large establishment, there was little time for individual attention and love. The directress of the home was reported later to have said that 'with some girls our orphanage worked and they were happy in it. But Norma Jean was not that sort of child.' However it was there that she learned how to apply make-up, which was kindly provided by the staff, and how to day-dream: an escape hatch from a reality which she resented very deeply. Occasionally, she asked how her mother was and was told a complacent 'fine'. But in truth, she was now virtually to be separated completely from Gladys. In later years she would rarely discuss her mother, perhaps feeling the same sense of betrayal that Charles Dickens felt when his mother put him to the blacking factory when he was young: he never discussed that painful time of his life and his only reference to it was sour and rancid as though the memory still rankled.

Part of Norma Jean's day-dreaming was of the movies, of course, because the or-

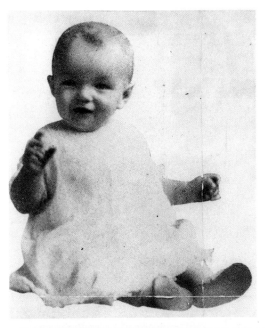

Two pictures of the young Norma Jean. On the left (reproduced from a newspaper photograph), the baby, and below, a happy portrait of the five-year-old Norma Jean taken in 1931, when she was living with her foster parents, the Bolenders.

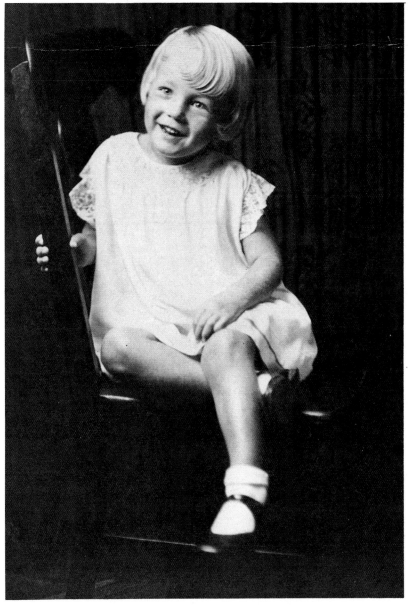

phanage girls were allowed to visit the cinema. She resented being called an 'orphan' because her mother was still alive, but she did not resent the cinema: that was a further exit for her from immediate reality.

Eventually came release. Grace McKee, an old friend of her mother at Columbia Studios, was appointed guardian of Norma Jean, and she went to live with Grace and her husband, Doc Goddard. She was asked if she wanted to take on the new name of her adoptive family, but never got round to doing so. In the Goddard family there was, for Norma Jean, some of the stability that had been so absent from most of her life. But, even under such secure wraps of family life, the rain came in.

Doc Goddard was a man who liked his liquor and was quite often inebriated. Norma Jean was fond of him, but aware that he could not be trusted entirely. Sure enough, one day he made what she considered to be a pass at her. There was a violent scene. Certainly, in later years, Marilyn dramatized it into a near-sexual assault and other writers have wondered just how far the pass had gone. That she was on friendly terms with him afterwards – just never letting herself be left alone with him – shows that it cannot have been the completely physical attack that she sometimes talked about.

Goddard's attention may very well have been attracted by Norma Jean at around this time, for she had burgeoned into a delightful and attractive adolescent girl. She was cute in a dimpled sort of way and she was only too well aware that her figure was of the kind that men and boys turned round to whistle at in the streets. War had broken out with Germany and Japan and pin-ups of Betty Grable and Alice Faye were the tops with servicemen; Marilyn has been reported as saying: 'I strove to look like Betty Grable, but I thought that Alice Faye had more class to her looks.'

The family were now living in West Los Angeles, with Grace's mother, Ana, and things seemed to be moving along as happily for Norma Jean as for other girls of pubescent age at that time. Events, though, now moved precipitately forward, occasioned by the fact that Doc Goddard had the offer of promotion and a job elsewhere. Other writers have said that Grace planned what was to happen now with cool deliberation, because she realized that Norma Jean would be a hindrance in the move to Goddard's new place of employment. Whether she did or not, the event was to mark Norma Jean's progress into a new aspect of life. And it concerned the old movie cliché – the boy next door.

Actually, Jim Dougherty lived a few doors away but he and Marilyn knew each other as neighbours. When Grace asked him 'as a favour' to double-date with Norma Jean for a local dance he agreed casually enough. Jim was very much the outdoor type, enjoyed all things to do with the fresh air. Norma Jean was happy enough to go along with that as their relationship developed. For it *was* developing. Came the time when Grace suggested to the elder Doughertys that the two of them were such an 'item' that they might as well get married.

Somehow or other, that was what was projected. Was it part of a deep-laid plot on Grace's behalf? Marilyn thought so when talking about it later. Whatever the truth, the fact is that on 18 June 1942 the marriage took place. The Goddards, who were by now in Virginia, were unable to come, but the Bolenders turned up. Norma Jean's mother, though, was absent, having been moved to a new mental home.

It is worth noting the ages of the bride and groom. He was 18 and Norma Jean was only just 16. Somebody remarked: 'Are they old enough to know what they are doing?' and somebody else answered: 'Well, it's wartime.' That was the all-purpose excuse.

Jim Dougherty was working at the Lockheed plant as an engineer, and the pressure was so great on production demands that there was no time for a honeymoon. Instead the newly-weds went weekend-fishing at Sherwood Lake near where they lived in Sherwood Oaks. They must have seemed a very ordinary couple, apparently very much in love, so that when Jim was put on night-shift at Lockheed, she would put a love-note in his lunch-basket so that the night would pass more quickly for him. But Jim had married a girl of sixteen, with a girl's looks and attractions of that age. As their marriage continued he became more and more aware that his wife was growing into quite a beauty: the envy in other men's eyes, when the two of them went to dances or, even, walked down the street was becoming oppressive.

That this niggled at him he was afterwards readily to admit. He had the feeling that others were to feel later: that Marilyn – Norma Jean as she was then – belonged to other people besides himself. And, in belonging to all she really belonged to none. But Norma Jean, certainly at that time, thought that their love could stand the invasion of other men's attentions, especially when those attentions were confined to frank glances of admiration for the way her body had developed. That relationship, though, was now going to be put to the test. And it was a test that it could not withstand.

Norma Jean in 1945, when she was 19 years old. Although she looks so young, she had been married for three years, was about to obtain a divorce and was already launched on a modelling career.

Jim Dougherty, feeling more and more conspicuous out of uniform, had joined the Merchant Navy as a physical training instructor, and, eventually, he was shipped out to Australia, later to Italy. The war had taken him away from Norma Jean's proximity. He left her behind with a collie dog, which she adored with the same lavish attention that she had bestowed on a mongrel which she had adopted but which had been shot by a neighbour when she was small. She moved in with Jim's mother and settled back to await the end of the war and her reunification with Jim.

But her mood, without Jim, was restless. She wanted something to do, perhaps even in a patriotic way to feel that she was part of the war effort of which Jim was in the front-line. So she got a job as a parachute-packer. It was simple enough work, but

Norma Jean brought such enthusiasm to it that she was graded by her employers as 'excellent'; it was not a grading which was all that much appreciated by the other girls on the factory floor who considered that Norma Jean – who was not all that talkative at lunch-breaks – was just that bit pushy, a bit above herself. Then something else happened which moved Norma Jean further above herself than usual. An army photographer happened.

It was an incident that has been thoroughly documented since. The photographer was David Conover and he was on an assignment at the factory to photograph working girls for *Yank* magazine. There was to be a plurality of females, but Conover's expert eye rested upon Norma Jean – and stayed there. His camera, over the next few days of photography, was exclusively upon

11

her. He was the first to realize just how natural the girl who would become Marilyn Monroe was before a camera: it was the beginning of a love affair with a lens that was to last all her life. Even the director Billy Wilder, who could be very critical of her working methods, said: 'She is one of those stars who bloom into beautiful life when she is in front of the camera. They have this mutual attraction, a mutual admiration society, which we, the audience, witness with gratitude.'

Another photographer saw those photographs that Conover took and, too, was impressed by her naturalness. He asked her if he could photograph her outdoors over a weekend. Norma Jean readily agreed. It was fun being so much the centre of the camera's attention.

Those outdoor photographs came to the attention of Emmeline Snively, who was then the boss of the Blue Book Model Agency. She asked Norma Jean to call and Norma Jean went. Would she like to work a week as a hostess for a steel firm at an Industrial Show? She would indeed. She took time off from the factory, without explaining why, and took over a stand at the show. It was in its way a minor triumph; never had a steel company had so many enquiries. The men flocked with their questions, happily satisfied with the answers supplied to them by this attractive young model.

That was the start of model work, which took off completely after the colour-spread in *Yank* magazine. For a time Norma Jean tried to combine modelling with her job

The sort of picture that was earning Norma Jean a growing reputation among the agencies as a magazine cover girl before she achieved her dream of being in films.

Any excuse was good enough for another stunning picture of the young Marilyn's curves. This unlikely shot of every boss's dream stenographer was taken in 1947, after she had been offered a contract by Twentieth Century-Fox.

packing parachutes, but something had to give and it was parachutes that were sent packing. It was as though Norma Jean had spent all her life waiting for the way her ambition could be defined. Now she knew in which direction her life would be moving. The elder Doughertys were not happy with the situation, so Norma Jean moved out. Her letters to Jim overseas were full of love, but even at that distance he must have felt some sort of disturbance about what was happening, because his mother had written that Norma Jean wasn't 'around all that much'.

When he came home on leave, though, all seemed to be well. He was aware that modelling had its dangers in the contacts with other men, but Norma Jean made it seem and sound as though he were the only man

who could ever be in her life. It made him feel more secure. The war was over but Jim was still circling the world on his freighter; he had two photographs of Norma Jean at the side of his bunk: they made her seem nearer.

It was, and perhaps he knew it in his heart of hearts, only an illusion. He said afterwards that he was 'half-expecting' what was about to happen. Norma Jean had already discussed her future with Miss Snively and had been told that top models could – if they were good enough – get contracts as actresses with one or other of the major film studios. It was then and there that Norma Jean decided that the broad direction in which her career was now heading could be even further refined to a single track – that leading to stardom.

Pictures of her protégée appeared on cover after cover of magazines; she posed for calendars; she learned the trade of knowing just how to look for the camera. She was, in a work-drenched sort of way, very happy.

She even went to studios for auditions, but nothing came of them. Then one day in July 1946 she went for an audition to Ben Lyon, the casting director of Twentieth Century-Fox. Lyon had been a film star himself, then a comedian – with his wife, Bebe Daniels – in Britain during the war. He had an eye for talent. He saw it immediately in Norma Jean. She was given a film test and Lyon recalled that the spark he had felt on meeting her was suddenly up there on the screen, but multiplied a thousandfold. 'She glowed; she was tremendous, although very nervous.' Norma Jean was offered a contract starting at 75 dollars a week. But there was one small point. Her name. It didn't sound right.

Lyon remembered a former entertainer called Marilyn Miller. Marilyn was an interesting name. Norma Jean was asked if she liked it. Only, said Norma Jean, for the last time Norma Jean, if she could couple it with her grandmother's name. Which was? 'Monroe', said Marilyn Monroe.

Above: The finished studio image of the young starlet. This photograph of Marilyn was taken after a make-up session at Columbia Studios for *Ladies of the Chorus*.

Right: A glamour shot of the early Monroe, making the most of her figure, taken around 1947–48.

Jim Dougherty received the attorney's letter while his ship was in Shanghai. A divorce was called for. The marriage, which had been quietly expiring, was over.

The reasons may be hard-hearted, but they were complete enough reasons in themselves: studios just did not sign up potential female talent if that talent was married. The reason: the possibility of pregnancy. A starlet, after all, was an investment for the future and business is business – a business which could not afford to let itself be swollen out of success and into bankruptcy by an act of nature which could be forestalled.

So the Doughertys were divorced. Norma Jean was 'orphaning' somebody else for a change. She who had all her life been left by one person or another, who later said that she had felt manipulated during all the early part of her life, was herself leaving another human being. It was a pity, but there it was. 'He was a kind man', she recalled later, 'but, you know, we had nothing in common.'

Meanwhile back at her career, Miss Snively was conscientiously applying herself.

Marilyn in 1955, wearing one of her costumes for *The Seven Year Itch* (Twentieth Century-Fox), with the studio's casting director, Ben Lyon, who had realized her screen potential when giving her a test in 1946.

THE GOOD MR HYDE

A new name? Perhaps Marilyn hoped that, along with it, there would be a new switch of direction to her life: that it would, at last, have some purpose against the feeling that dogged her all this early part of her life – and to some extent to the end of it – that she was either drifting or being manipulated. It was not to be, of course. Marilyn found, like so many other aspiring starlets around this time of 1947, that a film studio was a factory just as the parachute factory was, and everything was geared to the product. She wasn't part of, or involved with, that product yet. She was on the periphery of Fox's real activities.

Of course, as an attractive girl with an undoubtedly real and luminous personality, she made friends . . . usually men friends. Principal among these was Joseph M. Schenck, an executive producer at Fox, who at the age of 69 had a reputation for womanizing and a power which made him a formidable personality among those in the know on the Fox lot. 'He was a cute little guy', Marilyn was reported later to have said

of him, a description with which his enemies would have agreed only so far as the diminutive aspect of his appearance went. Cute, he wasn't – to them. But for Marilyn, who graced his dinner parties, he was a provider of at least some good meals.

Marilyn was finding that times were tough; the crock of gold at the end of the rainbow, that she had expected her contract to be, was buried too deep. Then came what was officially her first film, a role which was so fleeting as to be missed if you blinked. It was as a girl on a boat in a film memorably titled *Scudda Hoo! Scudda Hay!* (it was later changed to *Summer Lightning*), a rural hay-ride piece of nonsense which starred June Haver and such hayseeds as Walter Brennan. Natalie Wood got her name on the credits, but you have to look very hard down the cast list to find Marilyn's name. This movie was so distinctly uncelebrated that years later Marilyn could hardly remember what it was about. Similarly, *The Dangerous Years*, which followed (although it was released

This scene from the first film Marilyn made, *Scudda Hoo! Scudda Hay!* (Twentieth Century-Fox), was later cut from the movie. Marilyn and Colleen Townsend prepare to row away while Robert Carnes watches.

earlier than *Scudda Hoo! Scudda Hay!*), again had Marilyn in a small role – a few minutes longer, admittedly, but short enough – as a waitress serving some juvenile delinquents in a café. Thus she had gone along with two strands of cinema's post-war trends: the yearning for ruralism and the belief that anyone below the age of sixteen was up to no good.

Her own life, though, was conforming to no known direction apart from that which states that starlets must suffer as much as possible, so that when they attain the heights writers will have something to write about to explain that top-of-the-tree neurosis. Despite those Schenck dinners, which came albeit infrequently, she was often having to manage on one hamburger and a helping of cottage cheese a day. And even that diet looked as though it would be ended with the news that Fox were not renewing her contract, despite that friendship with Schenck.

However, he was to do her one last, parting favour before she shrugged off those Fox furs – which had turned out to be coney –

not for the last time, but certainly for what she thought then would be the last time. Schenck phoned his friend Harry Cohn, who was boss at Columbia, and said that Marilyn had something which Columbia might appreciate, especially as there was a musical, *Ladies of the Chorus*, being prepared. This, directed by Phil Karlson, was very much a cheapie about burlesque chorines and their offstage romances, and had such forgettable names as Adele Jergens and Rand Brooks in it. It was, however, to be the first film in which Marilyn's name was to figure somewhere up front.

Marilyn's experience of musicals was limited, in fact, to watching those starring Betty Grable or Alice Faye. She had simply no idea how to project that sexy whisper which was later to be amplified as so much a part of her personality. So Columbia assigned a vocal coach, Fred Karger, to help her. It was to become an emotional experience for them both, but from it came Marilyn's lifelong friendship with Fred's mother, Anne, a woman who was always to be her friend and

Marilyn as a waitress between former child stars Dickie Moore and Scotty Beckett in *Dangerous Years* (Twentieth Century-Fox), her first film to be released, although the second she made.

Prominent billing and prominent pictures for Marilyn on a poster for only her third film, *Ladies of the Chorus*, made for Columbia and released in 1949.

always to defend her against any charge of promiscuity. 'She thought of marriage as the natural outcome of mutual passion', she once said.

That it was not to be marriage with Fred was a cause for regret, although work on *Ladies of the Chorus* was so demanding that it drove much of that affair out of her head, as the chores progressed. It was a simple enough story, with Marilyn as the daughter of a burlesque star, who becomes a star of that particular stage in her own right – and then meets and falls for a young society playboy. But even such low-scale rhetoric requires some sort of professional approach. Columbia decided that not only did she require a vocal coach but a dramatic coach as well, Natasha Lytess.

All her life Marilyn was to feel inadequate as an actress, seeking help and guidance from others whom she deemed, rightly or wrongly, to have better knowledge of such things. Natasha Lytess, a grey-haired, dominating woman with a great deal of tough charm, was to be the first of these coaches in Marilyn's career. Miss Lytess admits, in her memoirs, that she took a good deal of interest in her pupils' private lives and tried

to talk Marilyn out of seeing too many men and to persuade her to wear underwear. She was also aware that at her first meeting with Marilyn the girl was 'utterly unsure of herself'. That she was late for the meeting was yet another indication of that lack of belief in herself – or was it, asked Miss Lytess, an example of an ego that would keep others waiting?

Some writers have suggested that, in Natasha Lytess and Anne Karger – as well as many of the others who were to make their way into her life – Marilyn was unconsciously seeking out the mother that she never really had or, at least, who was too remote from her, by way of mental illness, ever to have had any maternal impact. It is a viewpoint that makes more than a case for itself. Throughout her life there were always to be older women, as well as older men, who somehow or other shaped what was to be her destiny.

One of the songs Marilyn sang in *Ladies of the Chorus*, 'Every Baby Needs a Da Da Daddy', might equally well apply to the distaff side of parenthood as well.

Then, in September 1948, came disaster. Columbia dismissed her from the studios. The story, which it must be admitted Marilyn encouraged in later years, was that she had refused the advances of studio boss Harry Cohn, who had exploded into a ferocious display of anger that one of his starlets should thus repudiate him. Cohn's libido was as publicized, and as much a matter of studio concern, as L. B. Mayer's at MGM. If the story of Marilyn's rejection of him is true, there might well be good grounds – in Cohn's mind – for the girl being dismissed: if it got around to his fellow film-tycoons it might well be a laughing matter for them which would undermine his power. And power was the real name of the game: not the name of Marilyn Monroe.

Other girls might well be able to overcome such a wrench from an anchorage with little difficulty or, at least, come to terms with the knowledge that that is the way Hollywood is – especially for young girls out for a career. But Marilyn had had too many severances to take it all with that kind of equanimity. Natasha Lytess reported that Marilyn was distraught, even contemplating the aid of a psychiatrist or the Roman Catholic Church.

She was still very friendly with Natasha Lytess, even staying with her and her daughter at this time, but she was very depressed. There was always modelling work, of course, and it was at about this time in the autumn of 1949 that she worked with photographer Tom Kelley for the calendar that was later to add notoriety to her fame: she posed nude for a photograph that was titled

Marilyn in 1950, heavily made up as usual and wearing large drop earrings for her role in *As Young as You Feel* (Twentieth Century-Fox), one of her nine films which were released in 1950 and 1951.

'Golden Dreams'. But needs must, when the
devil of unemployment and the fact of fifty
dollars a day from Kelley drives.

Then she slipped back to Twentieth
Century-Fox almost unnoticed for a film,
starring Dan Dailey, called *A Ticket to To-
mahawk*. This was to have been a one-off,
but friends spoke up for her and she went
into a film called *Love Happy*. It did her no
harm around this time to find that she had
been mentioned in the syndicated gossip col-
umn of Louella Parsons, who wrote kindly
about her as a Hollywood orphan who had
been brought up within sight of the studios

– and whose ambition it was to go on working there.

Love Happy was an off-the-rails vehicle
for the Marx Brothers, a not very bright
example of their wonderful absurdity, all
about the difficulties – surprise! surprise! –
of putting on a musical. Marilyn's role was
small enough, to be sure – progressing sexily
into Groucho Marx's office and complaining
that she was being followed by men, while
he leered understandingly at her – but it was
to establish her as a presence in the eyes of
one man who was to be very important to
her at this time. His name was Johnny Hyde
and he was a very top-notch agent indeed.

Hyde was a talent scout. And Marilyn, he
told everyone, had talent with a capital 'T'.
He was also 'love happy' himself.

Johnny Hyde was later said by Marilyn to
have been the real reason she became a star.
He had a strong belief in her and fought to
have her recognized. Marilyn was extremely
grateful at the time, and always remained so.
What he did was at some sacrifice to himself.
Married with four sons – the eldest of whom
was about the same age as Marilyn herself –
he found his wife filing for divorce and some
of his friends believing that he was being
taken for a sucker by a scheming, younger
woman. He never believed that. As a vice-
president of the William Morris Agency, he
was an articulate, forceful man of some lit-
eracy and discrimination. He realized that
Marilyn, like others of his protégées had
been, was a woman who had not realized her
potential as a person, who lived only for
movies. He set out to groom her to be a star,

Above: The delectable good-time girl looking as innocent as possible in *The Asphalt Jungle* (MGM).

Right: All cameras, lights and action as Marilyn, lying on the couch, plays a close-up scene with Louis Calhern in MGM's *The Asphalt Jungle*.

helping her choose the right dresses and the correct costume jewellery.

In the film *Marilyn, The Untold Story*, Johnny Hyde was portrayed by Richard Basehart, and, certainly, in photographs of the time, Hyde can be seen to have some of the looks of the actor. But accounts suggest his personality did not need to be as forceful as Basehart's portrayal would have us believe. He was a very wealthy man and had many friends within the business. One of these friends was John Huston, the famed director, who was setting up a movie called *The Asphalt Jungle*.

This was a criminal caper movie of an unusual kind for the times in which it was released (1950). It told the story of the robbery from the point of view of the crooks themselves, characters varying in degrees of

intelligence but always viewed with some ironic sympathy. Sterling Hayden was the muscle-man, while Sam Jaffe was the mastermind, whose penchant for young girls leads him to disaster. Involved with them was the crooked lawyer Louis Calhern who, with a perpetually ailing wife, has a bubbly blonde of near-adolescent age as his mistress. This was the girl to be played by Marilyn in a movie which endeavoured to show that crime itself was but a 'left-handed form of human endeavour'.

Huston recalled that he had wanted to test Marilyn for his previous movie, *We Were Strangers*, but 'circumstances kept getting in the way'. He now tested her for *The Asphalt Jungle* and decided that her projection of insecure seductiveness was exactly right for the role.

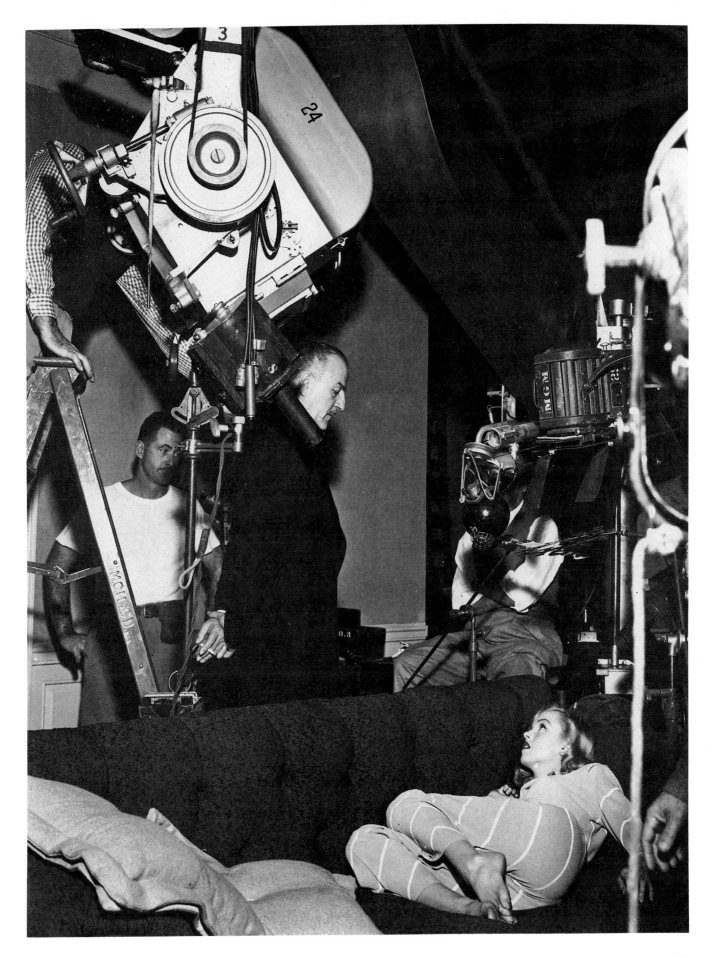

Marilyn played the small part of a guest at a theatrical party in the very successful *All About Eve* (Twentieth Century-Fox), and despite the galaxy of stars was widely noticed by the critics. On the stairs, listening with her to Gregory Ratoff, are Anne Baxter, Gary Merrill, George Sanders and Celeste Holm.

Perhaps he sensed in the part a kind of type-casting for Marilyn, in that she was involved with the distinguished Johnny Hyde, who was himself a much older man with a wife whom he loved. Certainly the performance given by Marilyn suggested more than just the 'bit' parts she had been used to; although small, it nevertheless carried a weight of impact. She was a motivation for the older lawyer to behave in the way he did; she was the girl who, unwittingly, caused him to self-destruct.

There were those, especially at the William Morris Agency, who thought the same motivation could be seen in the relationship between Marilyn and Hyde. He devoted practically all his attention to her, and during the years 1949–50 she completed around six movies with his help, some of which were negligible in terms of her career but all of which succeeded in helping her image in the public's eye. Perhaps one of the most important of these films was *All About Eve*. This literate and spiky comedy drama of life backstage is about the insecure great actress, played by Bette Davis, who feels her position eventually threatened by the ruthlessly aspiring Anne Baxter, who moves from sycophant to positive rival. At one of those larger-than-life theatrical parties at which people use aphorisms as, in olden times, they might have used rapiers, Marilyn turns up as Miss Caswell, brought by drama critic George Sanders.

Her role was that of a vacuous, on-the-make kind of girl whose overt hankering for a kind of fame was an exact opposite to the covert envy portrayed by Anne Baxter. Marilyn made enough of the part to ensure that critics noticed her, in a film that won general acclaim all around; Bette Davis later recalled that, although Marilyn was on set for only a couple of days, 'she certainly made herself felt. The stills photographers couldn't keep away from her when she was not in front of the movie camera, and she seemed to take great delight in their attentions. No, nobody was jealous of that attention; rather, we were amused. We were all of us, after all, older in the actual business of acting than she was, so we felt she should get the most publicity that she could. Besides, she was so modest when you spoke to her; I rather liked her.'

This was a sympathetic view which was very much opposite to that which the family and friends of Johnny Hyde took of Marilyn. The gossip columnists kept referring to the May-and-December romance, but Hyde would hear nothing against her. He furthered her career with a sacrificial ardour that probably compensated for the physical ardour from which he was severed by a series of heart attacks. He was by now a very sick man. Not so sick, though, that he could not induce Marilyn to have her nose 'bobbed'. That plastic surgery, he thought, was a physical touch which would finally make others appreciate her as much as he did himself. 'Some sweet kid', says Louis Calhern of her in *The Asphalt Jungle*. 'Some sweet kid', Johnny Hyde might well have reiterated in real life.

Marilyn's publicity photographs frequently pictured her outdoors on beaches, in bathing suits, wrapped in towels, or, as in this studio shot, making the best of herself with brightly coloured props like a parasol.

In her early films, Marilyn sometimes provided her own wardrobe, and this outfit, with the carefully arranged clip on the neck, had already been seen in *The Fireball*, when she made *Home Town Story* (MGM), with Jeffrey Lynn.

All this time Marilyn's personality *was* growing in the public consciousness, however; people were aware of her, even if they weren't quite sure about which movie they had seen her in. So big was this appreciation of her that the news that she was being considered for Grushenka in a new visualization of Dostoyevsky's *The Brothers Karamazov* caused interest not only in Hollywood but in the minds of the many men in the street who had so far only seen her as a platinum blonde with a breathy, sexy giggle and a way of walking away from the camera which was a whole scene in itself.

The role of Grushenka eventually went to Maria Schell, which Marilyn afterwards lamented, but Dore Schary of MGM, with whom Hyde had discussed the idea, had been interested – which presupposed that Marilyn was not to be merely simply restricted to mindless, if appealing, blondes. At about this time, November 1951, Johnny Hyde and she finally signed a seven-year contract with Twentieth Century-Fox which would be paying her 750 dollars a week within a year. Darryl F. Zanuck, the boss of Fox, had let it be known that he thought little of Marilyn's potential as a dramatic actress. But obviously he realized she was a product who could be sold, and that, after all, was what film companies were all about. It was as though this act of Johnny Hyde's was rushed through at his request because he realized that soon Marilyn would be once

more on her own, without his protection. That contract would provide a security which, without his being around, she might well need. So, having put her house in order, Johnny Hyde died of a heart attack on 17 December 1951, in Palm Springs.

Natasha Lytess, with whom Marilyn stayed at this time, felt that her charge should not be left alone, so grievously did she seem to be stricken by Hyde's death. Shock seemed to have concussed her with sandbag-force, so that she seemed to have difficulty in hearing questions that were put to her. She was sedated with pills too, pills which were later to become such an important, frightening part of her life. But at least, she said later, they 'helped me to sleep'.

Hyde, seemingly, had asked that Marilyn be treated as one of his family, but that was a request that the family could not tolerate. It was suggested that she would not be welcome at the funeral, but in fact she went along with some friends to say her last farewells. Her sobs were said by members of the family to have been in bad taste, but those who have followed her career might perhaps forgive her for what may well seem a brash mourning to others, for once again she was losing somebody she loved. Moreover, without his guile and charm to protect her, she was very much on her own. Her weeping might just as well have been for herself, and her own vulnerability, as for Johnny Hyde.

Above: Robert Mitchum, on the left, sizes up the dance-hall entertainer, played by Marilyn, in *River of No Return* (Twentieth Century-Fox), a rugged outdoor film shot on location in Canada.

Right: Marilyn at the premiere in 1953 of *How to Marry a Millionaire*. With her, from the left, are George Bowser, Humphrey Bogart, Lauren Bacall and Nunnally Johnson.

The reason for the horror shown by Marilyn and little Tommy Rettig in *River of No Return* (Twentieth Century-Fox) is a battle between Robert Mitchum, without his gun, and a mountain lion, on their flight through the north-west frontier wilderness.

She met him before she went on to make *River of No Return* for Otto Preminger. A double dating had been arranged, but she had forgotten all about it, arriving more than an hour later when reminded of its existence. At that time DiMaggio was the most famous baseball player in America, but Marilyn was not particularly interested in that, so conceivably she took him on first sight and as he was 'like a businessman, he looked so conservative; I expected sportsmen to be much flashier than he turned out to be.' It was a friendship that lasted some months, before it became marriage, but it brought

41

Marilyn out into the world again.

So much so that she was able to fight back when the irascible Otto Preminger ordered Natasha Lytess off the set of *River of No Return:* Marilyn went immediately to Darryl F. Zanuck and Natasha was partially reinstated. It shows something of the power that Marilyn realized she could wield, that she went straight to the studio boss – and that he agreed with her rather than the more senior Preminger. The film itself is no great shakes, with Marilyn as a deserted wife (!) hiring Robert Mitchum to bring back her husband. But it works well in terms of its own simple narrative. Nevertheless, Marilyn

was not happy with the kind of movies she was making at Twentieth Century-Fox and, with photographer Milton Greene and his wife, Amy, set up herself as her own company. That was on the professional side of her life; on the private side was her marriage to Joe DiMaggio, on 14 January 1954.

The wedding took place in San Francisco's City Hall with Marilyn wearing a fashionable, but conservative, brown suit at DiMaggio's request. The spectators were many and inquisitive. Everyone had eyes for Marilyn, but she only had eyes for DiMaggio. 'I may even retire,' she told the Pressmen. 'I may just do that.'

Marilyn kissing the man she probably loved most in her life, Joe DiMaggio, after their wedding in 1954.

A SUPERSTAR IS BORN

The first stop of Marilyn's and DiMaggio's honeymoon was Honolulu, the second was Tokyo. In both places DiMaggio became aware of just what kind of legend he had married. Mobs of fans ran screaming at the two of them – security had not been alerted – and the DiMaggios had literally to run for cover. DiMaggio was later to say it was the most frightening experience of his life. Marilyn, too, was reported as saying that she was terrified, but in a way it was an experience that was to help her in her by now antagonistic dealings with Twentieth Century-Fox. They had sent her a script of *The Girl in Pink Tights*, the script which she regarded as 'lousy', and rejected. The studio thought this was just a tactic to upgrade her contract and threatened action. The reports coming in from afar now made them realize that Marilyn was not just any actress to be kicked around at their discretion; she was, in every sense, a superstar, whose charisma crossed all frontiers, barriers and languages.

This realization was made even more evident when she decided she wanted to entertain the American troops fighting in North Korea. DiMaggio at first argued against it, but she won him over to her point of view and Marilyn made what can only be described as a conquest. Occasionally, there were what were reported to be 'small riots' among the soldiers anticipating her arrival. She sang, she danced, she generally cavorted for them, in all ways living up to the sexy Barbie Doll image that the studios, and to some extent she herself, had created. A writer in the *New York Times* complained that the troops had rioted wildly 'and behaved like bobby-soxers in Times Square, not like soldiers proud of their uniform'. But if Marilyn's appearances had raised temperatures, either with indignation or sensuality, she herself succumbed more physically on her way back to Tokyo and contracted a kind of mild pneumonia. It took her some days to recover, and then she and DiMaggio toured the rest of Japan. After all, they were still on honeymoon.

Then it was back to Twentieth Century-Fox and into her next movie – not *Pink*

On her honeymoon with DiMaggio, Marilyn stopped off to entertain troops fighting in Korea. It was against DiMaggio's wishes and he was taken aback by the adulation and applause she received.

Tights, but *There's No Business like Show Business,* a curious amalgam of schmaltz and absurdity with Marilyn as a sexy singer of saucy songs. She sang three numbers, 'After You Get What You Want You Don't Want It', 'Heat Wave', and 'Lazy'. It had a mixed reception from the critics. Bosley Crowther, of the *New York Times,* who had previously been an admirer of Marilyn's work, lamented her 'wriggling and squirming . . . which are embarrassing to behold'. But Frank Quinn of the *New York Daily Mirror* described her performance as 'sizzling'. You paid your money and you took your choice.

Marilyn's next film-choice was to be, in 1955, *The Seven Year Itch,* co-written by Billy Wilder, who also directed. It was a day-dream fantasy with Tom Ewell, without his wife for the summer, as the middle-aged

husband fantasizing about The Girl (Marilyn) who has moved into an adjoining compartment. It became famous, not to say notorious, for one scene in which Marilyn, standing above an air-vent in the road, has her flounced skirt blown high.

The occasion was filmed on location in New York and Joe DiMaggio came along, too. That he was dismayed by the sexy way his wife seemed to be displaying herself has been well noted. During the scene with the skirt flying upwards, watched by a crowd of people who had heard that the film was in production, he stood and watched with distaste. One newspaper reporter asked him: 'What do you think of Marilyn having to show more of herself than she's shown before, Joe?' DiMaggio did not answer directly, but walked away, his views evident

Above: *There's No Business like Show Business* (Twentieth Century-Fox), and Ethel Merman introduces her priest son, Johnnie Ray, to Marilyn.

Left: Marilyn oomphing it up in another scene from *There's No Business like Show Business* (Twentieth Century-Fox) as she does justice to her torrid dress and Irving Berlin's songs.

45

least show other professionals that she was up there with them in the major leagues. There was one hope, though, and that was in the film that Arthur Miller had written, which was called *The Misfits*.

The story concerns three ageing cowboys who drive wild horses out of the mountains near Reno, frightening them with planes, then rope them from a fast-moving truck and sell them for dog food. Marilyn's role: a divorcee who falls in love with the principal cowboy, yet is unable to understand what he does for a living. Miller's script shows the way the American pioneering spirit has been corrupted by commercialism.

Eli Wallach played one of the cowboys and Montgomery Clift another: he was a fine actor, of a self-destructive nature, of whom Marilyn said he was the only person she had met who was in worse shape than she was. She herself was in pretty bad shape, by now completely relying on tablets to get her up in the morning and to put her to sleep at night. Despite this she still suffered from acute insomnia. She promised, though, to try to be on time and not to cause any trouble on *The Misfits*, especially as her hero, Clark Gable, was playing the leading cowboy with whom she falls in love. Gable, 'The King', was already a legend when Marilyn was born; she remembered that she had fantasized that, in fact, he might have been her real father. Now, at 59, he was still a tough, charismatic figure, but, as he said, 'awful tired'.

Left: A rather mannish coat for Marilyn in *Let's Make Love* (Twentieth Century-Fox), but anything less masculine than its effect cannot be imagined.

Left: Perhaps their troubled lives drew Marilyn and Montgomery Clift together. Seen here in *The Misfits* (United Artists), they had a good relationship off screen.

Far left: One of the production numbers from *Let's Make Love* (Twentieth Century-Fox) was 'My Heart Belongs to Daddy', Cole Porter's standard. Marilyn proves she looks as good in a man's sweater as in anything.

61

Clark Gable was the idol of young Norma Jean before she became Marilyn Monroe, and Marilyn was thrilled to work with him in *The Misfits* (United Artists) and hurt when it was suggested that troubles in the shooting might have accelerated his death.

As scriptwriter, Marilyn's husband Arthur Miller was constantly on location for *The Misfits*, and indeed Marilyn is sitting in his chair, but she often ignored him, and their marriage was beginning to break up.

It was to be a nerve-wracking and gruelling film. Horses had to be ridden at breakneck speed – although stunt men were used closeups often called for the principals to do the riding – and Clark Gable had a bad back. And, despite her good resolutions, Marilyn was holding up the production with her lateness and illnesses which may well have been psychosomatic.

The director was John Huston, who had first worked with Marilyn on *The Asphalt Jungle* and knowing of Marilyn's reputation for being late on the set he had the daily call changed from 9.00 am to 10.00 am, to try to make things easier for her. It didn't. Clark Gable would drive out in his sports car, rehearse his lines then open a book. He never complained, no matter what time Marilyn showed up.

Although Marilyn seemed to be in a daze a lot of the time, she could also be wonder-fully effective. It wasn't so much acting, Huston thought, as dragging something up from her subconscious, something which looked marvellous on screen.

Huston, though, was only too well aware that Arthur Miller and Marilyn were on the verge of breaking up. 'One evening I was about to drive away from the location – miles out in the desert – when I saw Arthur standing alone. Marilyn and her friends hadn't offered him a ride back; they'd just left him. If I hadn't happened to see him he would have been stranded out there. My sympathies were more and more with him.'

As a director, he was far too honest about her talent not to realize how remarkable she could be. 'I never felt Marilyn's much-publicized sexual attraction in the flesh, but on the screen it came across forcefully. But there was much more to her than that. She was appreciated as an artist in Europe long

64

before her acceptance as anything but a sex symbol in the United States. Jean-Paul Sartre considered Marilyn Monroe the finest actress alive. He wanted her to play the leading female role in *Freud*.'

Marilyn was not so happy with herself, nor with *The Misfits*, which was around forty days over schedule and had been filmed in black and white ('you'd have thought they could afford colour'). The days after shooting finished were not happy for her either, as Clark Gable died in mid-November of a heart attack which some said had been brought on by the aggravation caused on *The Misfits*. The aftermath, therefore, seemed but a naturally gloomy extension to what had gone on during production. The reviews by the critics were, however, kinder than the circumstances surrounding the shooting. Said Paul V. Becker in the *New York Herald Tribune*: 'Here Miss Monroe is magic . . .

not a living pin-up dangled in skin tight satin before our eyes.' Another wrote: 'Hers is a dramatic, serious, accurate performance.' Balm for the wounds, but not balm enough. The marriage to Arthur Miller was now over. She felt that she had come away from the marriage with nothing; at least *he* had material for a play, *After the Fall*, which he was to write after her death.

It was, though, Twentieth Century-Fox insisted, time for work, under the contract by which she still owed them a film. *Something's Got to Give* was to be the title and its story was of a wife who returns from apparent death in a yacht accident to embarrass her husband (Dean Martin), who has made other plans for his life. Marilyn went to work with director George Cukor and one celebrated scene was shot in a swimming pool – that of Marilyn nude. It was to have been her 30th film.

Left: In her last, unfinished, film, *Something's Got to Give* (Twentieth Century-Fox), Marilyn allowed herself to be photographed nude for the first time since the infamous calendar session many years before. Here she has just emerged from the swimming pool.

Far left: Marilyn and Clark Gable bidding farewell to each other after the last scenes shot of *The Misfits*. This happy occasion for Marilyn soon turned to sadness, as a few days later Gable suffered a fatal coronary attack.

Marilyn was never happy with the script and her old habits of lateness began to re-emerge. Production stopped, and was never to resume. Then Twentieth Century-Fox did what nobody had ever thought a studio would do in the circumstances, knowing Marilyn's deepening neurosis. The company filed suit against her 'for wilful violation of contract'. It was a bitter blow. Marilyn went into deep seclusion and could only be reached by close personal friends such as the Strasbergs, who put it about that Marilyn was contemplating the stage and a role in 'Anna Christie'. Joe DiMaggio, with whom she had continued to be friendly after their divorce, was always on hand. And, of course, there were doctors. There were always doctors.

But on 5 August 1962, there was nobody around when Marilyn most needed them. There was evidence that she had tried to phone people, leaving her telephone number on doctors' answering machines. On a chair were some legal documents that she seems to have been reading; documents concerning her legal wrangle with Twentieth Century-Fox. But there were also, on the table beside her bed, bottles of pills. And Marilyn Monroe was dead.

The housekeeper, awakened by 'an uneasy feeling', found her at three o'clock in the morning. All over the world millions of people who had regarded Marilyn Monroe as standing for something bright and vital and part of their own lives found themselves in a state of shock. The coroner's report said that it was 'probable suicide'; certainly her dying was the result of an overdose of barbiturates. But those who take such pills know how easy it is to take too many; the mind cannot remember the count of how many have been swallowed.

All the judgements simply meant that a light had been snuffed out. The light that was Marilyn Monroe. And in Los Angeles Jim Dougherty said to his second wife: 'Say a prayer for Norma Jean. She's dead.'

Even after their divorce, Marilyn continued to have a strong affection for Joe DiMaggio, and often liked to be with him, particularly at low moments.

Right: Marilyn's funeral casket, covered with flowers, being taken from the chapel to the cemetery. The pallbearers are Alan Snyder, her make-up man, Sidney Guillsroff, her hairdresser, and four mortuary employees.

EPILOGUE

Marilyn Monroe was 36 when she died and *Something's Got to Give* would have been her 30th film. It was an ironical title considering what happened to her, and an irony at which she might well have giggled. It still seems incredible and unbelievable, remembering her on-screen personality, to believe that she is really gone from the cinema and the world. In his funeral address Lee Strasberg said of her: 'The dream of her talent, which she had nurtured as a child, was not a mirage. When she first came to me I was amazed at the sterling sensitivity which she possessed and which had remained fresh and undimmed, struggling to express itself despite the life to which she had been subjected.'

There was obviously something more than just physical beauty in her, something in her performances with which people identified. She had 'a luminous quality – a combination of wistfulness, radiance, yearning – to set her apart and yet make everyone wish to be part of it, to share in the child-like naiveté which was at once so shy and yet so vibrant . . .' She was a sensitive artist and woman who brought joy and pleasure to the world.

Joy and pleasure, of course, but, to a certain extent, after her death – guilt. As Fred Lawrence Guiles wrote: 'None of Marilyn's

Marilyn as guest of honour at an Actors Studio benefit party, sitting between her old friends Lee and Paula Strasberg.

Marilyn with her third husband Arthur Miller. She was a great reader, and it was once suggested, not wholly in jest, that her brains and his beauty made a good match.

friends, husbands and lovers escaped a profound sense of guilt that was to supersede for a time, and in some instances for all time, the warm memory of a young woman with laughter ready at her lips, a laughter sometimes wry perhaps, but none the less there.'

Yet the self-destructive pattern of her life made her early death seem inevitable.

Arthur Miller himself tried to erase Marilyn's memory from his own life with a play, *After the Fall*, in which the childlike actress Maggie is not unlike Marilyn. He regarded it, he said, as no more autobiographical than his other plays, but the critics were unanimous in seeing that Maggie and Marilyn were one and the same.

There were all kinds of theories regarding her death; that the Kennedys, John F. and Bobby, were somehow involved. But as Lena Pepitone was to write: 'It was, and has been, frequently whispered that Marilyn was having an affair with President Kennedy, or his brother Bobby, or both. Marilyn didn't get mad at these rumours, though. She just laughed. The Kennedys, whom she had met through Frank Sinatra's friend Peter Lawford (then the husband of a Kennedy sister, Pat), were "cute", Marilyn said. She liked them because they were funny and smart. "But they're not my type. They're boys." '

But, in a more general aspect, many who never met her in person felt that guilt; her audiences, even. As though somehow they had betrayed her. It was something she was aware of when I met her on a couple of occasions: this sense of treachery for some unspecified crime. She had been reading Kafka's 'The Trial' in which the hero Josef K. is arrested for a criminal act which is never described and of which he is not aware.

She was always a great reader, as if trying to catch up with her lack of real education, to fill in those gaping holes of which she was too much aware. Her comments on 'The Trial' when I met her at Egham were perceptive. 'It's like we all feel, this sense of guilt. I know they say it's the Jewish thing with Kafka – that's what Arthur (Miller) says anyway – but it goes beyond that. It's about all men and women. This sense that we have fallen or something. I suppose that's what they mean by Original Sin.' It was a strange conversation to be having with a supposed sex-symbol, but our interview was a strange one, anyway. People drifted in and out, not being introduced; the first time I met her was in the morning when she seemed tired and disorientated. The second was late afternoon when she seemed more composed and relaxed.

One of the matters which exercised her very much were the critics' reactions to her. She didn't need them, she said vehemently, but judging by the way she constantly returned to the subject she felt that they ought to need her. She admitted to a preference for Bosley Crowther, but that was all; the rest were just writing 'to make headlines'. But looking through 'The Films of Marilyn Monroe' edited by Michael Conway and Mark Ricci, the quotes of favour come early, surprisingly early, in her career. In her way Marilyn was always to some extent the Critics' Choice.

Even as far back as *Ladies of the Chorus* Tibor Krekes in the *Motion Picture Herald* was writing about it: 'One of the bright spots is Miss Monroe's singing. She is pretty and, with her pleasing voice and style, she shows promise.' Her prowess in *Love Happy* rated no comment at all, but possibly because everyone was too besotted with the Marx Brothers and their looney antics. *The Asphalt Jungle,* though, unleashed a few superlatives for Marilyn amid all the comments on the film itself. Liza Wilson wrote in *Photoplay*: 'This picture is packed with standout performances . . . There's a beautiful blonde, too, name of Marilyn Monroe, who plays Calhern's girl friend and makes the most of her footage.'

Mostly, for some time after that, the comments from critics were about the movies themselves, not specifically Marilyn. *Let's Make It Legal*, though, had Frank Quinn, of the *New York Daily Mirror* saying: 'Marilyn Monroe parades her shapely chassis for incidental excitement.' And Wanda Hale in the *New York Daily News* wrote of Claudette Colbert and Macdonald Carey: 'Their presences and a satisfactory amount of bright dialogue counteract strained farcical situations and the indifferent story . . . Marilyn Monroe is amusing in a brief role as a beautiful shapely blonde who has her eye on Zachary Scott and his millions.'

Perhaps the most eulogistic comment came from Alton Cook in the *New York Telegram and Sun* about her role in *Clash by Night*: 'Perhaps we should mention the first full-length glimpse the picture gives us of Marilyn Monroe as an actress. The verdict is gratifyingly good. This girl has a refreshing exuberance, an abundance of girlish high spirits. She is a forceful actress, too, when crisis comes along. She has definitely stamped herself as a gifted new star, worthy

Marilyn had only a brief role in *Let's Make It Legal*, but her name appeared on the advertising posters. She received good notices from New York papers, who found her exciting and amusing.

CLAUDETTE COLBERT
MACDONALD CAREY
ZACHARY SCOTT
in
LET'S MAKE IT LEGAL

WITH
BARBARA · ROBERT · MARILYN · FRANK
BATES · WAGNER · MONROE · CADY
SCREEN PLAY BY F. HUGH HERBERT and I.A.L. DIAMOND · BASED ON A STORY BY MORTIMER BRAUS
PRODUCED BY ROBERT BASSLER · DIRECTED BY RICHARD SALE

20th CENTURY-FOX